NO QUIZ 2019

HENRY WORLD SCHOOL

POEMS

BY

TRINIDAD SANCHEZ, JR.

with Introductions by
Evangelina Vigil
and
José Montalvo

Pecan Grove Press • St. Mary's University
San Antonio, Texas

Poems by Father And Son
Poems by Trinidad Sánchez, Jr.
Poesias de Trinidad V. Sánchez

Copyright 1996 © Trinidad Sánchez, Jr.

1984 - First Printing   1985 - Second Printing
Published by Renacimiento Press, Lansing, Michigan

1996 - Third Printing - This edition includes selections from the 1984, 1985 texts-poems of Trinidad and his father, into one volume plus introductions with some new poems.

           Karen Narvarte   Pecan Grove Press

2002 - Fourth Printing

All rights reserved. No part may be used in any manner whatsoever without written permission of publisher except for brief quotations used in critical articles or reviews.
Printed in United States of America. For Permission contact:

                    Pecan Grove Press
                    St. Mary's University
                    One Camino Santa Maria,
                    San Antonio, Texas 78228

Printed by: KIMCO ON DEMAND PRINTERS
4120 Brighton Blvd. Suite A 21, Denver, CO 80216

For additional copies write to:

Trinidad Sánchez, Jr.
3480 Grape Street
Denver, CO 80207
(303) 388-7638

ISBN: 1-877603-41-4

**Dedicated
to my sisters
Lila & Lucy
y mis hermanos
"Los Cepillos"
tambien
al Pueblo
en lucha
por su libertad.**

ACKNOWLEDGEMENTS

A mi querida mamá, Sofia Sánchez, who had the wisdom to treasure the poetry of her husband of forty-five years, and pass it on to me. She returned to be with him on March 8, 1996, having celebrated a full eighty-nine years.

I also want to thank deeply Karen Narvarte of St. Mary's University, a dear friend, whose interest in my work has encouraged me to reprint this collection of SON/FATHER POEMS.

I also wish to thank Ann Lozano, Anne E. Miller, Laura Sánchez, and Elizeo Lozano for their meticulous reading of the text and for generous suggestions, as well as Glasgowinandi Chandra for his time and patience in typesetting the manuscript.

CONTENTS

7 INTRODUCTION VOL. I By Evangelina Vigil
9 INTRODUCTION VOL. II By José Montalvo

I EN SOLIDARIDAD

13 HECTOR DE EL SALVADOR
14 DOMINGO XCOY HERNANDEZ
15 GABRIEL Y MARIA
16 WITNESS IN THE BELLY OF THE BEAST
17 GUERRILLOS (Pronounced: Gorillas)
18 THE RAIN FOR PARCHED LANDS
19 A TIME TO RAISE QUESTIONS
20 LA MUERTE
21 DEATH
22 I WANT TO DEDICATE THIS POEM
24 MONTEREY POOLROOM
24 PHOTO: POOLROOM
25 PHOTO: INSIDE POOLROOM
27 FOR PAPA
28 THE FIRST TIME
30 KILLING OUR FATHERS
33 CROSSING OF RIVERS

II ON BEING CHICANO

35 ON BEING CHICANO
36 PHOTO: CHICANO WITH TATTOO
37 CHICANO
38 ON BEING CHICANO II
40 ON BEING CHICANO III
41 ON BEING CHICANO CARNAL
42 THE STRUGGLE FOR CHICANO SURVIVAL
43 LA PLACITA
44 CALIFAS/CALIFORNIA
45 JOSE
46 CHICANO PERCENTAGES
47 TACOS A MI MANERA
47 LOVE
48 PHOTO: WOMEN WITH TRINO
49 MUJERES
50 A LOVE POEM

III DETROIT

51 THE BAKER STREET BUS
52 TWENTIETH STREET--DETROIT
53 FLIGHT 0293 TO ST. LOUIS 4/18/83
54 THE DREAM
55 LA DIFFERENCE
56 ANOTHER GREYHOUND POEM
57 LUCIO
58 FRANK MURPHY HALL OF JUSTICE (A Short Play)
59 FEET POUNDING THE SIDEWALK
60 UNANSWERED QUESTION
61 LA LLUVIA
62 WHITE-HAIRED WOMAN
64 PAY TOILETS HAVE YOU EVER CONSIDERED?
66 ABOUT TO WRITE A POEM
67 I THOUGHT YOU WERE A POET

INTRODUCTION VOLUME I

The "coming of age" of the Chicano people is a complex subject that will be written about for years to come. Ours has been a history of oppression which has affected many generations, dating back to the Spanish Conquest of Mexico and the birth of the Mestizo. Our parents have shared with us accounts of the prejudices that they have endured, and their parents have shared the same with them, and on and on.

The sixties and seventies vividly dramatized a crucial point of arrival for Mexicanos living in the U.S. virtually as second-class citizens. It was as if during this era the collective subconscious of our people was triggered by a sudden unrefutable realization of our victimization by an oppressive dominant society. With this arose a strong awareness of the urgent need to work toward positive changes. The role of the contemporary Chicano leaders became one of commitment to a lifelong struggle for social equality, for spiritual and intellectual liberation.

It is understandable that this weighing history should have a significant influence on the thinking of sensitive writers and artists of Mexican American descent. The vestiges of outright racial discrimination remain and abound in our present society, as does the actual practice. The contemporary writer whose focus is the Mexican American experience has this history to deal with, as much as the dynamic present and the unveiling future.

Trinidad Sánchez, Jr. is one such writer who feels compelled to communicate the social experience of his people. His adult life has been greatly influenced by the Chicano Movement of the sixties and seventies. This popular movement addressed pressing social issues, such as racial discrimination, police brutality, the lack of equal educational and employment opportunity, the Vietnam War and political oppression. His poetry reflects the anguish and pain, as well as the vitality and spirit of a generation of Mexican Americans who managed to break through that stereotype image of the docile, complacent, uneducated Mexicano.

Many of Sánchez' poetic moments occur within political contexts. Some are humorous, some realistically absurd. Some are moving and painful--as in that moment wherein he cries for all the Jose's, whose lives are determined, cut off by the concern, love, care of insensitive others who are convinced that "they know best." His compassion for humanity is apparent, not only in his writings, but also in his commitment to helping those in need. As a Brother of the Society of Jesus, his work has exposed him to the plight of many in this country and abroad. In his poetry one can see a strong identification with the political struggles of the people of Latin America. It is the pain and suffering which builds strength and nurtures faith, he notes. And it is this battle for social justice that unites Chicanos with other third world people.

From his father, the late Trinidad Sánchez, Sr. a published poet, Sánchez has learned of the power of the written word as well as an appreciation for wit, humor and human understanding. Love and respect and a high regard for the family and other values have been passed on from father to son by way of example. The poet's choice to make his father's poems an integral part of this book reflects a loving, meaningful relationship between father and son and within the family. Their contrasting poetic sensibilities reflect two distinct generations. Of note is the elder's eye for aesthetics and his poetic capability of transcending the socio-political realities of his time.

Trinidad Sánchez, Jr. is a sensitive human being who has seen so much. Yet, he lives for more, so much more. "Forty and haven't seen enough," he proclaims. The poet's words impart what is close to his heart. His straightforwardness and honesty compel the reader to understand.

Ms. Evangelina Vigil is a fellow of the National Endowment for the Arts. A widely published writer, Ms Vigil has been recipient of a national award for poetry of the Coordinating Council of Literary Magazine. Author of a chapbook *NADE Y NADE*, published by M & E Editions in 1978, and *THIRTY AN' SEEN A LOT*, published by Arte Publico Press in 1982.

INTRODUCTION VOLUME II

AND:
   In the beginning, He/She, created the heavens and the earth; the earth was a formless wasteland, and the darkness covered the abyss, while a mighty wind swept over the waters.
Then,
   He/She said:
"Let there be light," and there was light. When He/She saw how good it was, He/She separated the light from the darkness. The Light was called day, and the darkness night.
Then,
   He/She said:
"Let there be a dome, and the earth, and the sea, and vegetation with plants and trees." And when He/She saw how good it was: evening came, and morning followed.
Then,
   He/She said:
"Let the earth teem with an abundance of living creatures: let there be birds that fly, great sea monsters, cattle, and creeping things. Let there be wild animals and creatures of all kinds." And when He/She saw how good it was, the animals were blessed.
Then,
   He/She said:
"Let us make men and women, in our image, after our own likeness."
And yes:
   He/She created humans, male and female, in the divine image, and blessed them, saying: "Have domain over the fish in the sea, the birds in the air, the plants and cattle, and all the living things that move on the earth.

   Evening came and morning followed the sixth day.

   On the seventh day while resting, He/She realized that the very last command was being abused. Siesta was interrupted, and He/She said: "Let there be Chicano Poets with conciencia, who will look after, and speak for those too small, too poor, or too weak to stand against the tyranny and oppression of those ungodly images who do not respect fraternal laws, nor divine love."

It is out of this very last divine command, that Trino's poetry is written, these unpolished social cries for justice, for brotherhood and love. Without justice, brotherhood or love, humanity cannot claim the divine image which was solely reserved for them.

For Brother Trino (like most of us), it took "women" to show him how to love, because we men are too stupidfied and apendejados being machos--or too busy hunting each other down--to show love.

Like "Gabriel and Maria," I am sure that Trino too is, a "marginado," only because he performs that divine duty of speaking out against atrocities and injustices; because even in "A Time to Raise Question," he demands: A Tribute for Peacemakers!

Even while giving thanks and seeking blessings for his meal, Trino speaks of solidarity with the children of the "Divine Being", (who has not forgotten them, but certainly ignored them), for they are too ignorant to read the word of "God." B.T. damns death, though death is the only one who seeks us equally--brother, grandmother, dad, friend: All..."all dead."

Trino questions rituals (baptisms) and the Mountains of Califas: the first, for becoming a show for technology; the later to see if they would hide anyone seeking liberty. He is aware that "La lluvia," the rain, does not wash away injustice, pain, hunger, and the loneliness that love and life can bring us.

His poetry goes beyond his own backyard, for he also hears the cries of other--blacks, who also, "have a dream," or hillbillies, too poor to enjoy the finer things in life, who must also like most greasy me-...chanics and other blue collar workers wait for Trailways bus drivers. Besides, flying might make one ask why airlines serve Danish Rolls, instead of Mexican Sweet Bread.

Trino also asks with inquisitive authority if anyone can be "TOO CHICANO." He voices our constant "Struggle for Survival" in deciding between: tamales or hamburgers, mariachi music or hard rock, molcajetes or blenders. He cries for Chicanos to stand up together, without looking down on others who must also fight for their survival.

"Frank Murphy Hall of Justice" could very well be a bayou in Houston, the I.N.S. along the Mexican border, the Silver Dollar bar in Los Angeles, a cross burning in Alabama, or a boatload of Haitian refugees sinking off the coast of Florida. The streets of Detroit are not much different from the streets of San Antonio, Tucson, Albuquerque, Denver, Chicago or New York, where pleasant things can happen. You have to be on the constant lookout, though, for those heartless souls who feel they have a "Manifest Destiny" duty to perform.

Trino's cynical bigotes can also sing about the commercialization and pompositfication of Christmas, Thanksgiving and baptisms, without losing the sensitivity to say a kind word about his friends Maximo, Joe Tobin, Florentino Cruz. He also makes other less life-threatening observations about cockroaches, and prayers that only come out of thirsty lips asking for poems when they are chapped. His main concern is for the meek to inherit the earth.

In the meantime, Brother Trino will continue to write and to create; he will only rest--on the Eighth Day.

José Montalvo
San Antonio, Tejas
January 11, 1985

José Luis Montalvo, born in Piedras Negras, Coah. Mexico. José became one of the outspoken poets of the Chicano Movement. Know as 'The Black Hat Poet,' he is author of *"BLACK HAT POEMS," "A MI QUE!," "PENSAMIENTOS CAPTURADOS," "THE CAT IN THE TOP HAT* by Dr. Sucio (A.K.A. José Montalvo)," and *"HOUSE FULL OF FRIDAS."* After living with cancer for three years he died August 15, 1994.

I EN SOLIDARIDAD

HECTOR DE EL SALVADOR

The calm voice
telling your story
on foot from Mexico City to Chicago
then Detroit, the Ambassador Bridge
final destination--Canada,
only to be caught by U.S. immigration.
Relating el dolor del pueblo
aterrorizado by Yankee guns.
Wombs ripped open,
fetuses pierced by bayonets,
then thrown to the dogs!
The pain,
el llanto de aquellas madres,
is ringing in my heart.
How many times
have you shared your life
with this story?
Listening with empathy to understand
your hypnotic calm--patience of a Job.
We spent that evening, watching the tv-program:
REAGAN ON HIS RANCH.
Crazy, for a moment
tears welled up in your eyes...
the anger in you wanted to lash out
for like so many Salvadoreños,
you understand...he is a murderer!

As our eyes met,
you looked down to an empty space
so as not to let me notice--
the calm had disappeared.

11/27/81

DOMINGO XCOY HERNANDEZ

I arrive with the fifty others to listen to your story.
The chair next to Máximo is empty.
Yours are striking Indian features.
Queche-Maya your language.
Máximo whispers: You've spoken Spanish
for only three years. It's impeccable.
You explain the Yankee government
is responsible for the horrors,
senseless death in your homeland.
Your soft voice distracts my thoughts
of your strength, familia, loved ones
and your desire to continue on . . .
where is the source of your energy?

Exiled, returning home is difficult.
Then the question: *Will you return?*
With conviction, without hesitation, you respond:
Sí, voy a regresar, mi vida es mi pueblo.
My frustration--the little I can do--annoys me.
A collection nets ninety dollars,
which cannot relieve the pain,
struggle and death you have endured.

You accept Máximo's invitation
to *Fuente de Elena's* for a simple diet--
menudo, corn tortillas y cerveza.
The woman with the hemorrhage
touched the cloak of the Master
for healing. I press against you
to take strength from your frail body,
at the same time taking in
your belief, your compromiso
a la lucha Guatemalteca!
¿Cómo aguantas? I nervously ask.
¿Qué es lo que te anima?
Leaning forward whispering,
as if to tell a secret you say quietly
Mis compañeros que han muerto.
Then recalling their deaths,
tears flow on your cheeks.

GABRIEL Y MARIA

Insisting the stories
must be told, told and retold.
You spoke of the massacres
San Miguel . . . how the Guardia Nacional
in the darkness of the night
brought together invalids/marginados
bullets extinguishing their lives.

Recuerdas que el pueblo
no come pescado (do not eat fish)
because the guardia nacional
throws the dead bodies of young
Salvadoreños into the rivers.
Or the time on the way home
the bus suddenly stopped,
gente running, moving
in the direction of the hill.
You join them, not knowing
it will lead to young men,
children who have been dismembered
by the Guardia Nacional.

The woman que se volvió loca
porque la Guardia Nacional, in her sight,
murdered seis hijos one by one!
Pueblo aterrorizado, marginados
los pobres without voice miles away.
In a soft voice you share
your questioning the mothers,
women who left their children behind
to escape Guatemala . . . until that solemn day
when the Guardia Nacional knocked on your door.
This story is interspersed with remembrances . . .
you recall each of your nine children by name.

I am left alone thinking of my nephews
on maneuvers in Central America!

WITNESSES IN THE BELLY OF THE BEAST

Julia, Omar, Francisco
poet, prophets denuciando injusticias
de Guatemala me causan lagrimas a oír
de aquel sufrimiento que ustedes conocen.

The audience Latino, Chicano, Hispano.
Attempting to draw attention to his question,
the reporter prefaced his remark:
I AM MEXICAN AMERICAN!
What does it all mean?
His attempt at survival in a city like Detroit
blinded him to la lucha de nuestro pueblo
en America Latina.

Julia, Omar, Francisco
the spirit of your story challenges us
to believe we can control our history,
we can change the injustice for a better life.
Our struggles are connected.
The strong Hope, Love and Faith
for your compatriotas is the GOOD NEWS.

Mexicano turned into Hispanic
by moving out of the barrio
up to the Heights, Birmingham,
the good life, wife, familia,
nice cars, education,
yuppie reputation.
Is it your fault?
No te das cuenta del sufrimiento
del pueblo pobre, our family,
the family we do not know
sufriendo una miseria,
un momento doloroso.
No entiendes.
Tienen derechos de vivir. No sobrevivir!
El llanto de aquellas madres
nos llega como el viento del tormenta.

Te invito a solidarizarte con ellos.
They must not stand alone in their struggle.

GUERRILLAS
(Pronounced: Gorillas)

NEWSWEEK, TIME MAGAZINE
calls them guerrillas--
son hombres y mujeres de paz,
pueblo en lucha por su libertad.

NEW YORK TIMES MAGAZINE,
SAN ANTONIO EXPRESS
calls them guerrillas--
son un pueblo de esperanza
construyendo una sociedad nueva.

CHICAGO SUN TIMES, DETROIT NEWS
calls them guerrillas--
que otras piensan que son comunistas,
pero son victimas del gobierno Yankee.

TELEVISION, RADIO, THE MASS MEDIA
calls them gorillas--
son el pueblo en marcha
unido y en solidaridad.

Algunos de nosotros call them gorillas
Apesar de que sabemos bien,
que son los pobres y los marginados.
Their real name is:
    raza noble, raza bronce
    hermanos, hermanas,
    madre, padre,
    los niños,
    más que todo son:

¡COMPAÑEROS!

THE RAIN FOR PARCHED LANDS

The rain upon the window

gentle sounds

reminding me of the weeping

of the mothers

searching for their loved ones

los desaparecidos . . .

más fuerte el sonido

of the rain upon the windows . . .

the tears of loved ones--

los desaparecidos

weeping for their mothers. . .

somewhere along the journey

the weeping/the tears

turn to sounds of gentle streams

bringing new life

to parched lands.

A TIME TO RAISE QUESTIONS

National news: Alex Ortega, "Hispanic"
was killed in Lebanon, reportedly his death
a tribute to all HISPANIC AMERICANS.
He was not alone, the others were Johnnie,
Juan, Danny, Randall, Ronald, Louis, Richard,
Rafael, Camera, Gómez, Garcia, Hernández,
Ortiz, Quirante, Rodríguez, Silvia and Valle.
. . . reading such lists make me reflect
on family who have joined the military.

His death raised the question:
Why do we not honor those
who believe in justice/peace,
refusing to go into foreign lands
to kill innocent people
for presidents and generals?

What keeps us from honoring those
who have given their life
to better educating themselves
returning home to their barrios,
to make it a better place
for the unfortunate, the poor?

We must honor those
who have refused to take up arms,
choosing more creatively to use
their talents for the kingdom.
Let us recognize those
who did not go to Lebanon,
who strongly believed
this is not the way to bring about peace!
Death of Raza is a time for tribute to Raza,
our brothers and sisters.
It is also a time
for all of us to raise questions
about our participation in wars,
the annihilation of peoples
for the interest of a few--the rich.

LA MUERTE

Al final
la pinche muerte;
ese momento de la vida
en que no hay vida,
y todo se vuelve
en recuerdos

Lo discutimos harto,
tu hermano, mi abuela,
tu abuelo, mi papá,
una amiga
todos muertos
de distinta manera.

Hablamos y hablamos
y menos entendimos;
cuentos de los antepasados
nuestra historia.
Futuramos
de nuestra muerte
cómo lo queremos
celebrar
sin estar presente.
Música,
trago,
alegría,
buenas memorias . . .
nadie llore.

Al final
la pinche muerte;
ese momento de la vida
en que no hay vida,
y todo se vuelve
en recuerdos.

DEATH

Finally
damn death,
that moment in life
when there is no life,
and all becomes
memories.

We discussed it a lot,
your brother, my grandmother
your grandfather, my dad
a friend
all dead
in very different ways.

We talked and talked
and understood less.
Stories of our ancestors,
our history
We futurized
of our death;
how we would want it
celebrated
without being present.
Music,
whiskey,
happiness,
good memories . . .
and no one cries.

Finally
damn death,
that moment in life
when there is no life,
and all becomes
memories!

I WANT TO DEDICATE THIS POEM

To mama, papa, my six carnales
affectionately known as Bozo or Cepillo,
to my sister Lucy and the Mellados,
my sister Lila and the Silvas,
to tios Fermín and Albert
my tías Odila, Lucy and Margarita
my primos in San Antonio and Eagle Pass
my nephews and nieces.
I'm a great uncle un chingo de veces
so I include my great nephews and nieces.
Can't forget my compadres and classmates
Ed Boyer, Bob Páramo, Benny Diaz and
to the sister who taught at St. Fred's,
especially the one who said
I couldn't write poetry!
Allow me to dedicate it to several Jesuits
Lou Lipps, John McGrail, Gus Scharf
Louie Puhl, Louie Aowad, Hank Kuhn,
Frank Malek, Bernie Wernert, Nick Predovich,
Charlie Sullivan and Bob Maat;
the 20th Street Jesuits, Bill O'Brien
Joe Mulligan, Ed Bobinchak & Bob Scullin.
I want to dedicate it to compañeros like
Rubén Solís, Roberto Piña, Willie Velásquez,
David García, Pauline, Sandra, & Blanca García.
Must not forget the Chicanas
like Sylvia Sedillo, La Gregory, La T.J.,
Maria de Jesus y Carmelita Montalvo.
And that crazy dude--Manuel Flores.
Vi, Cristy, and Máximo, I dedicate it to you
and the Team for Justice,
to my carnales members of H.A.S.T.A.
at Jackson, Michigan, to all pintos,
especially all those who are not mentioned here,
las que están en mi corazón.
You know who you are!

The final dedication
is for a Chicana poet,
muy de aquella--Evangelina Vigil
who published a book of poems entitled:

THIRTY AND SEEN A LOT.

The poem, I'm dedicating is entitled:

FORTY AND HAVEN'T SEEN ENOUGH!

MONTEREY POOLROOM

¡BOLAS! ¡BOLAS!
One table to the next
racking balls, racking them tight.
It's busier at night--only four tables
ten cents a game. ¡BOLAS! ¡BOLAS!
Automatic return tables were not a fad,
si me recuerdo bien, if I remember right
automatic pin setting was invented
about the same time.

¡BOLAS! ¡BOLAS! ¡BOLAS!
There was something, tu sabes,
professional, high class
to have someone rack your balls.
¡BOLAS! ¡BOLAS! ¡BOLAS!
Games ending simultaneously
kept you on your toes.
Nine ball (3,9 & 5) is the money game.

¡BOLAS! ¡BOLAS! ¡BOLAS!
It was a song, a drum beat
the batos banging cue sticks on the floor
while screaming: ¡BOLAS! ¡BOLAS! ¡BOLAS!

Only God knows how many tables
one could rack in a night
. . . does not seem like information
needed in heaven.
Remember the encueradas--
nasty old calendars, papa took them down,
when the priest came to play billar.
Pubic hair, there was something wrong
for the priest to see her naked!

¡BOLAS! ¡BOLAS!
Papa was professional, loved his work.
spent mornings shining the balls
He had to have them shining,
cue sticks sanded down, worn out tips
replaced, tables always clean, tears
on the gambling green always repaired.
¡BOLAS! ¡BOLAS!

Dreamt a lot about the future . . .
Would I do this all my life?
THE MONTEREY POOLROOM
Would it be part of the last will and testimony?
Wouldn't be a bad business, you know,
2nd, 3rd, 4th generation pool players.

¡BOLAS! ¡BOLAS!
No. It wasn't meant to be.
At sixty five he returned
to the Great Poolroom in the sky.
¡BOLAS! ¡BOLAS!
Fixing cue sticks, free pop, jukebox,
mexican records, changing pool table cloths,
rolls of new green felt. The pinball machines
near the window, the wooden floor full of cracks,
fluorescent lamps above each table,
the dirty windows, the nasty calendars,
have all become memories.

FOR PAPA

    Tonight
papa came to mind
    to my soul
    tonight
    a night
I feel lonesome and blue.

". . . it was papa who took a drink
    and wanted to hug you tight."

Tight, tight, tight
    tonight
will you hug me
    tonight?
tight, tight, tight.

Papa understood how
    tonight
I would feel lonesome and blue.
    Hug me
    tonight
take away the loneliness
that is so within
take away the blue
    tonight
    hold me
    tight.

I want to tell you, Papa
    tonight
I love you, Papa
    tonight
I want to hug you tight.

1962

THE FIRST TIME

. . . you tell your father "I love you"
is not easy. For we are taught
to love women. . . not men.
My father was the one I wanted
to be near, to feel his strength,
to know his passion for life.
The distance between us went unnoticed
until that fateful day--the phone call.
It would be my first airplane ride
from Cincinnati to Detroit,
ironically, to be with him at death.
Funny, for years I saved the ticket stub,
not sure whether to remind me
of my first flight or his death.

Standing next to him,
I remember being strong--
after all, I was his namesake
and others were expecting me
to be a man.

The day I cried was months later,
when I went to my mailbox
for his weekly letters and poems.
The box was empty--no letter, no poems.
I was so alone. Lost. Confused.
I had been taught about sex,
but no one had explained
the overwhelming sensations
that arrive with the death
of the man who for twenty years,
I called "Papa."

He lay so still, properly embalmed.
His amigos from the Monterrey Poolroom
paid their final respects.
The priest said some stupid prayers.
I cursed God for the strange feeling
of being a young man without a father.
I wanted to hug him one last time
or would it be our first?

The line from the poem
he wrote to me, after my leaving home,

"it was Papa who took a drink
 and wanted to hug you tight"

floated around
like a bad taste in my mouth.

Now the distance between the family
has separated us
to different parts of the country.
Mama lost her voice.
She quietly waits for your return
at the Nightingale Nursing Home.
She teaches us a lesson--how sometimes
death sneaks slowly up on you,
weakens you till your last breath.
Now I struggle to be a father
for my beautiful ten-year-old daughter.
You are not here but I want you to know
I don't blame you anymore.

The poet in me wants to share a poem
with you, make you smile, laugh
but all I can do is tell the children
". . . my father was a poet."
I feel so proud at the precise moment
when I express your words with my voice:
but I remember too well,
how the first time I told my father
"I love you" was not easy.

7/26/93

KILLING OUR FATHERS

for Mario David Sánchez

Mama always said
I was going to be the last child.
She let papa name me "Jr."
Without really stating the fact
she was making it clear: she was tired.
She did not want any more children.
Was she practicing birth control?
I was number nine . . . almost 18 months later,
January 19, 1945 (to be exact),
we celebrate your birthday.

On my visits
to the Nightengale Nursing Home
my heart knows mama is waiting.
She was waiting for someone else.
Yes, waiting for you to forgive her . . .
waiting to ask for forgiveness.
I wanted to lie: *"Mama, I saw Madio.*
He said: Tell mama, I still love her,"
but Mama is the one who taught me not to lie.

You ran away.
Promised yourself never to return.
Every now and then your calls for money
told us you were still alive somewhere
and life was still treating you harshly.
We wanted to give you more than money,
but the static on the phone
kept you from hearing our words.
Your silence grows with the years.

One time,
I could smell the strong scent of alcohol
on the phone; but I could not tell
how long you had been crying.
I'll never forget how,
"I never felt connected to mama"
tumbled out of your mouth.
Your words finally express your torment.
I feign at understanding the pain.

That wasn't enough, you then blurted out:
*"I want to call mama
         and apologize for killing papa!"*

Your confession stunned me
woke me from the night stupor.
I stood up. I knew well enough,
papa died in bed, reading the paper.

Then explaining,
how during that intense moment
standing next to the bed,
you could not remember
papa ever touching or holding you.
The absence of his cariños
kept you from placing the nitro-glycerine,
his doctors prescribed, under his tongue.

I then realized how important it is
for fathers to touch their sons, to hug them,
to tell them that they love them.

In between our sobs,
My body throbbed with emotions.
I wanted to hold you in my arms, forgive you.
I wanted for you to forgive yourself.
I wanted to touch you like a brother
my soul ached for you to feel my love.
Explaining death broke my silence;
uncertain I really understood my own words;
but remember repeating several times:
it was not your fault, papa died.
It was not your fault, papa died,
 but I'm not sure what you heard.

My memory fails me. Were you a pall bearer?
Where did you sit in church?
Were you with us at the grave site?
Questions that quietly hang between the lines.

I want to call you Bozo, Cepillo,
names of affection,
I want to tease you, call you out,
the way your girl friends did on the phone:
Is Maaarrrio there?

More than anything I want to repeat,
Madio, I miss you, I love you.
I want to call you home, where you belong.
Yes, I want to call you home where you belong.

March 5, 1996

Por un falso paraíso
soy ahora Americano.
Si el destino así lo quiso
por dentro, soy Mexicano.

Trinidad V. Sánchez

CROSSING OF RIVERS

The conjuntura of dreams
forged from the journey
   in the heart
   inside your body
   with the hunger
   eating at the stomach
   against the heat of the sun.

Crossing of rivers
which no longer stand as barriers.
The desert did not dry up
the promises on your tongue
nor the thirst/desire
for the false paradise.
The conjuntura of dreams
born out of the marriage
of untested love
charted your path--
a new history.
Crossing of rivers
conjuntura of dreams
unlike the crossing of your heart,
the crossing at railroads
the crossing of anger.
It was a journey . . .
river water nourished blessings
you shared with others on the path.
The memory strengthens us
who continue walking
in the footsteps of my father,
who is unable nor likely to return
to the verdant false paradise
he left as a legacy.
July 1995

II ON BEING CHICANO

ON BEING CHICANO

I recall the monjas telling me
"Tomorrow you must wear green,
remember, it's St. Patrick's Day!"
I refused.
My first revolutionary act.

My body flushed, the pinche fear
she would flunk me,
or would get even because
I refused to turn IRISH!

On television, I was bombarded
to bathe with IRISH SPRING--
A MAN'S SOAP.

The swimming pool -
as soon as I entered the water,
the vato in charge of the pool appeared
pouring in a gallon of bleach,
because I refused to use IRISH SPRING.

Being Chicano is not easy!

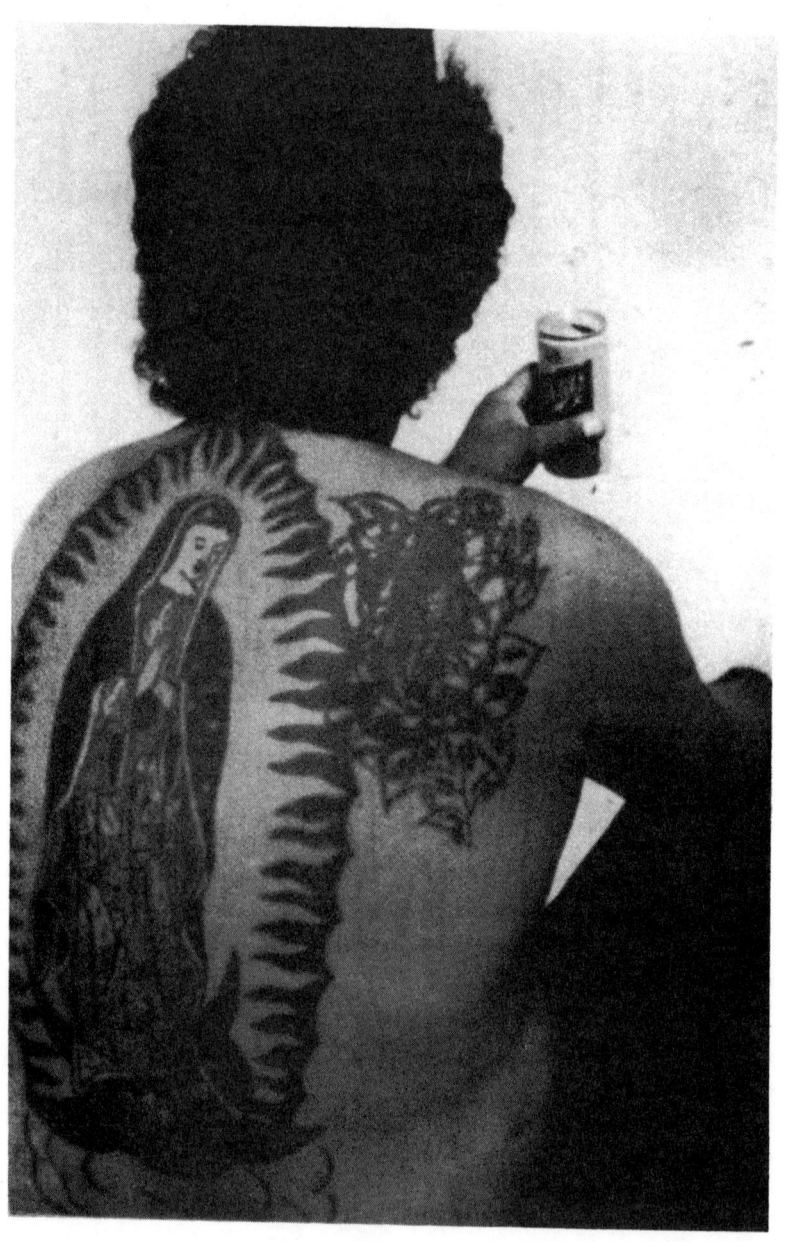

CHICANO

Hey, Chicano! Stand up!
It's your turn to be counted.
Raza needs you,
el pueblo te necesita.
Come out of hiding!
Take a stand.
Organize to take control
of your destiny.
Stand in solidarity
with your carnal,
tus hermanos/los niños!
Brother,
you don't stand alone.
It is in standing together
we are strong.
The world is ours.
Who are you waiting for?
Someone else?
Come out
from behind those drugs
the man is selling you!
Hey, Chicano!
Our people are in struggle
en marcha/on the move.
Look at the crowd--
You are not there!

**STAND UP
STAND TALL
STAND TOGETHER
STAND FREE!**

ON BEING CHICANO II

Today is the day I'll never forget.
Others would say: I'll always remember!
Pues de cualquier manera--
you'll understand why I write about it.

Today, I was fired for being
TOO CHICANO!
When I asked the boss
"What does this mean . . .
being too Chicano?"
He did not know nor could he explain.
Was I a Chicano too full of beans?

It was this moment in life
I wanted to caucus
with the movimiento brothers & sisters
who had taught me to be Chicano.
Ahora sí, they had never explained
that a Chicano could be **TOO CHICANO!**

For sure, I was angry and confused.
I didn't know whether to cry or to laugh!
Had anyone every been fired
for being **TOO IRISH** or, tú sabes,
TOO CZECHOSLOVAKIAN!
Imagine the boss saying:
"Sorry, Stephen, you no longer work here
YOU ARE TOO CZECHOSLOVAKIAN!"

At home, I stood in front of the mirror,
trying to decide if **TOO CHICANO**
was being **TOO DARK** or **TOO PANZÓN!**
Maybe he didn't like my T-shirt which read:

I'M
BILINGUAL - BICULTURAL
BISEXUAL - BIPARTISAN
&
BY
MYSELF

Quizás, he thought I was eating
too many frijoles or huevos rancheros.
Again I stood close to the mirror,
looking to see if being
      TOO CHICANO
might be a contagious disease.
That night I called my compadre
no le dije nada.
I wanted to check it out,
maybe being too Chicano was contagious!
Now either because he was too healthy
or too Puerto Rican,
he did not catch what I had. However,
we did catch a little buzz on the cerveza.

Maybe the boss did not like my bigotes
and was afraid to tell me he was jealous!
At a national meeting in D. C.
la secretaria instead of taking
the minutes for her boss
spent the time sketching my bigotes
in her notepad.
This is one of those memories I enjoy!
Maybe she was fired . . . I never heard.

Now, I know some raza
who are not Chicano enough.
I never thought I would lose my job
for being **TOO CHICANO!**
Pues, this poem does have a happy ending
not the Hollywood type,
Robert Redford would not fit the part . . .
the next morning after bathing
with IRISH SPRING, and fully dressed . . .
I went out and found a job!

ON BEING CHICANO III

A dream . . .
a dream came to me
from whereever dreams are from
the cosmic atmosphere
the other life
the beans.
It was a short dream,
one I'll never forget . . .
I had become a capitalist
president of a multinational corporation
whose product is a man's soap called:

¡CHICANO PRIMAVERA!

ON BEING CHICANO/CARNAL

Mama said: There are no such words!
Dónde sacas esas palabras: Chicano/carnal?
Mama is Mexican. She knows I am too.
But, Mama did not see my carnal last night
when through the beer in his eyes
he promised me he was through drinking.
He no longer wanted to live on the street,
living from curb to curb.
He wanted to make something of his life,
something his mamacita made him promise
before she died.

Nor had Mama seen the Chicano
struggling con las dos culturas
on the street, problemas con familia.
The booze, glue-sniffing was the pits.
La cerveza did not damage the brain as much
or so he thought.

Mama was not there when he broke down
because there wasn't any more hope;
she was not there to watch him take a chance,
trusting someone who was serious
who had offered to help.

Flashback . . . Chicago . . . the Mejicano,
upon our meeting, recalled Papa,
the Monterey Poolroom on Wilson Street,
how one Thanksgiving Day
Papa took him home,
shared mama's cooking, turkey con frijoles.
Ashen-faced, he spoke of his dilemma:
no food, no house, nothing.
Papa took him home.
Now he is a successful business man
with his own family living in Chicago.

Papa and Mama did not call him
Chicano/carnal in those days,
but they understood what it meant.

THE STRUGGLE FOR CHICANO SURVIVAL

can be an economic one or between cultures--
being American or staying raza!
No easy struggle, it's the difference between:

    Español or English
    menudo or corn flakes
huevos rancheros or pancakes
    tortillas or Wonder Bread
    quesadilla or grilled cheese
    tacos or bologna sandwich
frijoles refritos or navy beans
    tamales or hamburger
    chorizo or breakfast sausage
    salsa picante or President Reagan
    un cariño or a Hallmark card
    un baile or watching Dick Clark
    un abrazo or shaking hands
    un molcajete or an Oster blender
una revolución or a Democratic primary
being bilingual or being monolingual
    being raza or being Hispanic
being de la unión or a strike breaking scab
being Chicano or Irish on March 17th
hechando un grito or singing in the shower
    tata Dios or the almighty $$
    bien macho or domesticated
    bien bigotón or hairless
mariachi music or hard rock
Jarabe Tapatío or break dancing
ten folks in a Volks or two adults in an R.V.
    the Diez y Seis or the Fourth of July
    puro Mejicano or assimilating
    las mañanitas or Happy Birthday, Baby!

LA PLACITA

Hundred & hundreds of brown faces
(Mexican) the church is packed,
the padrecito hearing confessions
(listening to tales about sin)
for several hours at a time.

Fifty baptisms at one session
Thirteen thousand a year.
Baptismal certificates run off
on a computadora.
Fifty niños baptized
the final blessing given
the padrecito declares:
"SEE YOU NEXT YEAR!"

The pagans baptized
the real ritual begins
to Kodak the baby with
Koda-Color, Pentex,
YaShika, instant replay
self-developing,
Koda I & Koda II
Nikon, black and white,
color prints, slides
video cameras.

Babies baptized
fototized
camertized
movietized
digitized
computerized
mounted
matted and framed . . .
brings me to ask:

Did you register them to vote?

CALIFAS/CALIFORNIA

Califas tus montañas preciosas
bien altas y negro de noche
horizonte claro y azulado
pájaros volando.
Flores rojas-amarillas y de oro
en su primavera.
¿Si viniera una revolución
esconderías a los guerrilleros
en tus entrañas;
apoyarías los esfuerzos
de aquellos que buscan su libertad?

Califas, tierra santa, tierra robada
entenderías la lucha
de ese pueblo sufriendo,
de aquellos que no están libres.
¿Tus robles viejos daran sombra
a los cansados?
Te has convertido en mónstruo
comercializada,
computadorizada,
industrializada,
negociada,
K-martizada,
Hollywoodizada,
bankizada,
imperializada,
McDonaldizada,
Wilsonizada!

Califas un día regresarás
a conocer a tu pueblo--
los indios, los campesinos,
pobres, profetas,
revolucionarios, poetas,
pensadores del mundo nuevo
donde hay justicia!
Califas!

JOSE

The name did not really matter.
One of several brothers,
thin was his frame,
always answering the phone or door
with a gentle, welcoming smile.
His fifteen years were pure,
untouched by the real world.
The impressionable twinkle of his eyes,
windows to his soul,
revealing his love for familia.
The sister, his teacher, agreed.
She spoke of the big cake
he once made for a birthday at home . . .
then her cold, hard, ugly words:
"José will not make it."
stuck in like a knife!
Clearly, she meant no harm.

No sh..! I thought,
and wanting to scream
GIVE HIM A CHANCE!
Say: He'll have a hard time;
say: It won't be easy;
say: He may need some help;
but don't negate his potential!

José entered the room again.
Tightly taking his hand, I smiled,
grateful this handsome young Chicano
had not heard her remark.

On the way home
I saw the countless children, chicanitos,
whose lives and futures have been determined--
cut off, denied by cold, hard, ugly words,
disguised in a teacher's
love and concern.

CHICANO PERCENTAGES

Te has dado cuenta como los
Norte-Americanos
hablan de percentajes así:

14% of Texas voted in the election
02% knew of the poll
07% chance of rain
15% rise in crime
40% unemployment.

Chicanos on the other hand
translate percentages así:

95% = un chingo de gente, la mayoría*
85% = hubieras visto la cantidad
75% = eran muchos
60% = eran bastante
55% = pues casi la mitad
50% = la mitad
40% = unos tantos tontos
30% = pues igual como del otro baile
10% = eran poquitos**
05% = bien poquitos
01% = ni pa' hablar, la minoría.

*La mayoría son esos que siempre cuando les preguntas si van asistir a la junta, la conferencia, el encuentro, dicen: ¿Cuál Cursillo?, Cuál junta, a mí no me invitaron, ni supe.

** Eran poquitos (the chosen few) who are always invited to the cursillos, juntas y encuentros.

A recent Gallup Poll indicated casi la mitad reading this would agree with this poem. Another 25% would disagree and 25% would have no opinion!

TACOS A MI MANERA

Tortillas, frijoles
Aguacate y queso,
besos apretados,
¡Bien sabrosos!

LOVE

Love comes to town
Flashbacks
warm feelings
memories . . .
of affection
tenderness
love shared,
phonecalls.
What will it be like?
Will we have time
to be together?
Will it be like
old times?
We set a date
miscalculate.
Love leaves town.

MUJERES

Comprometidas con la raza
a los pobres, for a better life
for justice, afirmativas,
no se rajan, fuertes y de lucha.

Las simpáticas, sencillas,
con una sensibilidad
a los dolores del pueblo sufrido.
Las que ríen y saben zapatear . . .
gozan de la vida y sonríen
y a la vez son madre/padre
hermano/hermana
esposa fiel/compañera.

Mujeres de fé,
las que creen en Dios
y la Virgen de Guadalupe.
Bien valientes,
compartiendo sus vidas
en solidaridad
con los que luchan.
Honestas: algunas Chicanas
otras Puertorriqueñas, Latinas
negritas y güeritas.

These are the women in my life
the women who have shown me
how to love!

A LOVE POEM

Wanted to share my love,
not leave a mark,
words failed to express
emotions repressed.

She spoke of relationships
being hurt, of not understanding.
That was not what I was about.
What I didn't say was left unsaid.

A long time ago
I gave my life to Jesus
that's too damn easy to say.
Jesus--who is Jesus?
Is He her,
is He the wino
begging for a peseta,
the brother in jail,
the people I left in San Antonio?
Not quite.
Somehow my mind is explaining
things I should feel in my body . . .
it was an intellectual discussion.

Twoscore, a body not that old.
Carnal, she loved me y pues yo--
I did not read the signals.
So I write a poem
about being in love,
Jesus, and not understanding!

III DETROIT

THE BAKER STREET BUS

The bus trip home
was a ride of memories
for the old man to my left.
The sight of the buildings
as we turned toward Lafayette St.
gave him new energy, he felt alive.
He wanted to talk about it.
Didn't matter who I was.
With a twinkle in his eye
smile on his face
he spoke of his work fixing windows
40 years ago . . . before I was born.
As I look out and up
before another building
blocks the view,
his short glance tells me
the windows--well, the windows
needed repairs, glass, caulking.
The bus came to a stop.
The old man took his turn
carefully made his way
to the back of the bus to exit.
Sitting in the half-empty seat
his life reflected on the window
replete with the history of Detroit.
Tomorrow
we'll have more time
to exchange stories on the bus ride home.

TWENTIETH STREET--DETROIT

It's a neat place in the 'hood,
Place for gardens, not fancy.
We share lives, meals;
we pray--not easy at times.
Winter is around the corner,
the plastic on the windows
keeps the cold out. We believe.
We hope it won't be a hard winter
but prepare for the worst.
Others don't understand
how we live on this side of town
without maids/cooks and libraries.
It's a quiet street
under the Ambassador Bridge.
We've not been robbed.
What would they take--
the poster of Pancho Villa,
Archbishop Oscar Romero or Grenada?
Our Red White and Blue beer?
How un-American!
Dogs, we have our share, unjustly so.
Dogs, when let out to do do-do
do inform the whole neighborhood.

FLIGHT 0293 TO ST. LOUIS   4/3/83

Poor people never fly.
I love to show up
in worn-out jeans
sin mi corbata (minus my tie).
Today, I'm wearing my
"QUEMIRASPENDEJO" hat!
Appropriate enough, but
these folks are not bi-lingual,
my message falls on silent eyes.

Everyone carries a briefcase
full of computers/important papers
on how to make money--
I carry a knapsack full of poems,
dreams and plans for liberating prisoners.

Strong feeling of guilt move in on me.
I shouldn't be flying, tú sabes.
In flying you miss the barrio--
the South-End, the gas stations
without toilet paper, raza,
hitch-hikers.

One item the bus does not have:
"Safety Instructions," like planes
with the photo of people calmly climbing
on inflated rafts after a plane
crashes on the water!
Do they think I'm pendejo!
Mama, if this jet crashes,
you can be sure it will not land
so neatly on the water.

"Coffee, Tea?" "Coffee, please."
Plastic food, no pan dulce . . .
well something they call "Danish rolls"!

That's done . . . one hour to St. Louis.

THE DREAM

He had a dream
he had a dream
one day
Blacks/Whites
living together
in peace.
He had a dream
he had a dream
cut short
by a bullet
now a memory,
a page of history.
He had a dream
Yes, oh, yes
he did dream,
some people
don't understand
how dangerous
it is to dream.
He had a dream
one day justice
would reign
we would live as
brothers/sisters.
He believed in his dream.

Dreams are dangerous
when the poor
believe, trust, love,
and are committed to them.

LA DIFFERENCE

Carnal, ever notice la difference--
those who drag ass into Trailways
and those who run into an airport?
It's the smell of smoke
son las familias, los niños--
never do you see this many children
at an airport . . .
it's gym shoes, old clothes and ghetto blasters.

The pinche bus is three hours late
not much to do, bus stations
no tienen long hallways,
tú sabes, to walk up and down, so
I stand and stretch. Three hours,
qué hice to deserve this!
Raza, Mexican, Mexican-American
Black, Brown, American Hillbilly
and the vato loco with the camisa
that reads: **I MAY BE SLOW**
          BUT I'M IN FRONT
               OF YOU!

It takes all kinds, la ruca
in the tight jeans, the flowery blouse
eating a humburgesa, chismeando on the phone
is a vato loco, had me fooled!

Sí carnal--los bus stations son locos--
raza loco from all over
converging on the same point . . .
y lo que duele, what really hurts
is que a lot of people are going nowhere!

"MAY I HAVE YOUR ATTENTION
MAY I HAVE YOUR ATTENTION
CONNECTIONS FROM SAN ANTONIO
AND ALL POINTS NORTH."

You have my attention, bozo,
I've been waiting three hours for this bus!

ANOTHER GREYHOUND POEM

5:30 AM Today's Detroit Free Press read Motown does not have enough homes for the homeless to protect them from the cold weather and city council is concerned.

5:45 AM It has been a long time since I found myself sitting in the Greyhound station and rediscovering where the homeless come to hide and it's not cold outside.

6:30 AM Missing your bus is not as easy as you think! The ticket clerk insisted the bus to Cleveland was announced. Years ago, I wrote about the people who gather at bus stations without tickets or any place to go. This three hours of waiting reminded me times have not changed, only the aches and pains of my body now in its fourth decade.

6:45 AM The security guard approached the man asleep on the chair a few feet away, "May I see your ticket?" Some foul mouth words were spoken in response, to no one in particular, but loud enough for everyone to hear, something about city council! The words became lost with the security guard repeating in a more commanding voice, "**May I see your ticket!**" The homeless now carry fancy suitcases full of dreams in order to look like discriminating travelers, whose destiny is calling thus giving them permission to sit in this section marked **FOR TRAVELERS ONLY!**

7:15 AM This undiscriminating guard then turned and asked me for my ticket! He did not want to confuse me with some homeless soul without a ticket or is it that he suspected my duffel bag to be full of dreams instead of poems.

7:20 AM Having been identified as an official traveler with my ticket in hand, I was not sure what I would do if the migra showed up . . . in my hurry not to miss the bus, I left my birth certificate at home.

7:30 AM Two more hours for the next bus to Cleveland.

LUCIO

On the way to work
at corner of Trumbull and Bagley
the traffic light stopped me.
He walked over pleading
to take him to the hospital . . .
the detox center was what he needed
it was his bad cruda.
He needed to dry up. He was alone.
Andale, get in. I headed home.
He did not say much, I didn't pry.
Warmed up the beans & tortillas.
The huevos rancheros surprised him.
the coffee helped his hangover.
His smile told me he enjoyed it.
He admitted being a long way from home--
el valle en south Texas,
without any familia in Detroit.
I wouldn't waste my life con este frío,
but I was without the cash to fly him to Texas.
After breakfast he asked:
¿Me prestas una cachucha?
Gave him my new red, blue cap
He needed it more than me.

On my way to work, a week later
approaching the same corner.
The red, blue cacucha, it's Lucio!
Don't turn red . . . don't turn red . . .
my telepathic mind does not work.
The light turns red! Lucio waves.
He recognizes my Nova or is it me?
I pretend not to see him--
no tengo tiempo, I'm late for work.
Lucio tapping at the window,
"¿No tienes 80 centavos que me prestas?"
Eighty cents, that was easy.
I thought he wanted breakfast.

FRANK MURPHY HALL OF JUSTICE
(Poem to be dramatized)

JUDGE: Mr. Gonzalez, do you have anything to add or delete from the presentence report?

INTERPRETER: Yes, your honor, Mr. Gonzalez wishes to state, to clarify the reason he left Cuba is because he found the system so oppressive!

JUDGE: (Smiles)

COURT PERSONNEL: (All the Smiles reveal their views that Fidel Castro is bad and communism is bad).

INTERPRETER: Your Honor, Mr. González also wishes to say that what he didn't know is that it is just as bad here!!

JUDGE: (Banging his gavel on the bench.) Mr. Gonzalez, this court
finds you guilty of the charges brought against you
by the people of this state and sentences you to five to fifteen years in prison!

THE END

FEET POUNDING THE SIDEWALK

Poor people marching.
Everyone, including the old man
carried a protest sign.
Feet pounding the sidewalk
on this cold bitter day.
Judge Guy was inside
warm, drinking coffee, too busy
to listen to the poor people.
Feet pounding the sidewalk
their voices chanting
RELEASE THE FOOD
RELEASE THE FOOD
RELEASE THE FOOD
RELEASE THE FOOD
Feet pounding the sidewalk
with chants becoming louder
WE WANT A J O B
SO WE CAN E A T!
WE WANT A J O B
SO WE CAN E A T!
Feet pounding the sidewalk
RELEASE THE FOOD
WE WANT A J O B!
Me doy cuenta que I'm the only Chicano
Where are the Chicanos?
No doubt they'll be here
when the food is passed out.
Feet pounding the sidewalk,
bitter cold, folks hurting, new faces,
same feet pounding the sidewalk.
The seventy-year-old man
with a cane pounding the sidewalk
became a sign of hope.

UNANSWERED QUESTION

**WHY
DO WE KILL PEOPLE
WHO KILL PEOPLE
TO SHOW THAT
KILLING PEOPLE
IS WRONG?**

It was a button Michael wore
convinced as he was
"the death penalty was not
the way to deal with life!"

Ironic . . . our lives are penalized
with the death of friends
committed to justice and who love life.

> Family, friends
> young and old
> gather for farewells/good-byes
> to Michael . . .
> to bear witness
> that in their lives
> they have known
> a man of justice
> a man of God.

Death brings us together
to sing, pray and ask questions
to be answered
by those left behind.
Questions
Michael wore on buttons
and burned in his heart . . .

For Rev. Michael McGough
5/5/40 - 7/20/85

LA LLUVIA

Por la autopista I-75
cayó la tormenta y lluvia fuerte.

Me dí cuenta que el agua
hiba a limpiar las calles, y sidewalks,
the dust on the trees, the flowers.
The farmers would love the rain
reaching into the dark earth.
The plants would even love it more.
The wetness washed away
the mugre of splashed 'squitos
on the windshield.

Fuerte la lluvia y por un momento
I had hoped it would wash away
the suffering and hunger in the world;
of the poor, and friends in jail.
If only it could wash away
the ugliness, oppression, loneliness,
the betrayal men feel knowing
loved ones turn to others.
La lluvia--it was not meant to be
the wet/coolness smelled fresh,
it was over.
As a child I would play in it,
now I wanted it to perform miracles
to do so much more.
Trees, bushes a dark Nicaraguan green.
Flowers blossomed in their fullness
the earth quenched of her thirst.

It wasn't meant to be.
Injustice, pain, hunger, suffering
loneliness would remain--
it could not be washed away.

WHITE-HAIRED WOMAN

For Sr. Joanette Nitz, OP

White haired woman
daughter of farmers/Wisconsin
years have made you
quiet, prayerful, wise.
Friend, sister, mother
to so many who were without hope
lonely, lost, friendless.
Without fear you shared
life, laughter, gentleness, love.
The first time you needed
directions to the jail;
it was the incarcerated,
and the conditions of the jail
that changed your life.
Confronted by the ugliness,
smells of oppression/pain
of your black brothers/sisters,
the poor
you begin visiting prisoners.

White haired woman
understanding their lives/stories
you move to become part of them
to advocate, to stand with them
for change, for justice.
Your anger at the conditions
made you dream, one day
liberty would be proclaimed
to the captives,
prisoners would be set free
the poor would share the GOOD NEWS.
You've called others
to share your compromiso/commitment
with the many in jail/prison.
You have also touched our lives
we will never be the same.

Fifteen years of jail ministry
not an easy struggle
like the white haired women
of revolutions
you remain a sign of hope
truly a compañera!

Introducing you becomes difficult
for words fail to express
to capture your life . . .
I found I do it better with Spanish
  . . . una mujer comprometida
de las más comprometidas!
For the many who never returned
to thank you
for those who found gratitude
difficult to express
for all of us here tonight
we thank you for your life.

White haired woman
take your rest
reflect on those years.
Enjoy them. Pray for us,
that we carry on your task,
that we remain strong.
If I can glance into the future
to time eternal, for a moment
I'm sure when you meet your Maker
Jesus will say:
White haired woman--¡Compañera!
Bienvenida--Welcome.

PAY TOILETS
HAVE YOU EVER CONSIDERED?

For the Persons who asked: *Are you Mr. Pay Toilets and How do you say caca in Spanish?*

A poem about pay toilets.
Oh shit, you say!
Did you ever stop to think
how only in the U. S. A.
to caca do we pay? Or
it would be a better world
if instead, all of us were paid
ten cents to go caca?
Could it be pay toilets
are for the rich, their egos
to help them spend their money,
to separate poor people's caca
from THEIR caca!

What makes pay toilets different . . .
silver toilet paper, free markers
to write you phone number, gold seats?
Consider what archaeologists will say
thousands of years from now
when they dig up these pay toilets.
Could the government be distinguishing
between Democratic and Republican caca
or is big brother taxing your caca?
Possibly people who prefer pay toilets
think their caca is better than yours?
Pay toilets may have different plumbing
to separate the sophisticated caca
from the ordinary caca!
Wait! **IT'S OUT OF ORDER.**
There isn't any toilet paper!
Consider for a minute
how "North American" pay toilets are . . .
when your only change is a Canadian dime.

Oyes, on second thought
la señora crawling under the door
could be your sister, a **PH.D.**,
a banker, **YOUR CARNAL?**

STOP RIGHT THERE!
You think I'm crazy, pero bien loco
writing poems about caca . . . correction,
this poem . . . is about pay toilets . . .
I think pay toilets stink!

ABOUT TO WRITE A POEM

Hey Shit!

What's this cockroach
doing on my typewriter?
Does he think he is a poet?
Is he writing a letter home?
Is he telling his little brothers
what a great place it is
this 20th street!

Could it be a reincarnated
Chicano/Chicana returning
with the secret to make me
a famous poet or to tell me
how to write a poem about
cucarachas!

That will be the day!
¡Qué loco!

WHAM! Got the sucker!

I THOUGHT YOU WERE A POET

Write a poem about it . . .
I said: *NO I WON'T!*

That would make a good poem!
I said: *NO I WON'T!*

What a great idea for a poem!
I said: *NO I WON'T!*

Why not write a poem on it?
I said: *NO I WON'T!*

It's material for a good poem, he looked at me.
I said: *NO I WON'T!*

Surely, this is a poem!
Why is he calling me Shirley?
I said: *NO I WON'T!*

You can't miss this opportunity of a poem!
NO I WON!T!

Do you call this a poem?
NO I DON'T!

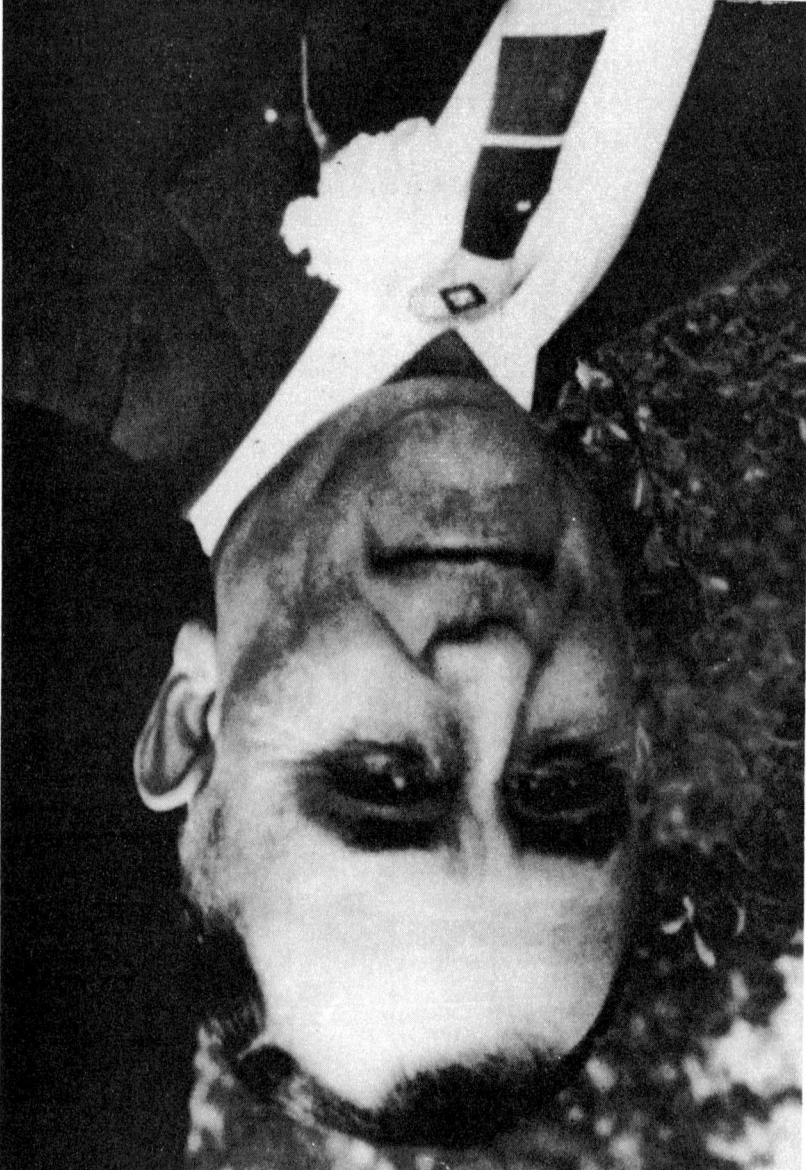

IF YOU COME BACK

The castles I have fashioned
in dreams beyond compare
have now begun to vanish
leaving nothing but despair.

The road I take is longer
seems like it has no end.
without rhyme or reason
my fondest hopes descend.

My heart once warm and tender
now feels an icy chill.
No matter how I try I fail
to capture the old thrill.

To say I am blue without you
can only part explain
the yearning deep inside my heart
that fills my life with rain.

The clouds no longer carry
me up to the stars on high
and life is dark and empty
because you said good bye.

Perhaps some day I'll rebuild
those castles in the sky
if you come back some day
I know for sure I'll try.

SI ACASO VUELVES

Los castillos que formé
en los sueños de mi vida,
todos se evaporaron
y hoy me encuentro perdido.

El camino está mas largo
nos separamos los dos,
cada paso es más amargo
desde que dijiste Adiós.

Mi corazón estaba tierno
ahora frío y muy duro
mi vida es un infierno
mi camino más oscuro.

Decir que sin tí, estoy triste
es solo explicar, una parte
la vida no tiene chiste
vivir y no es un arte.

La nubes ya no me elevan
a las estrellas, cerca de Dios
y las musas ya no me elevan
cuando me dijiste Adiós.

Pero un día, vuelvo a formar
mis castillos en el cielo
siempre te voy a esperar
pues ya sabes que te quiero.

ALMOST

As she brushed past me
My heart turned a summersault,
She could almost kiss me
As easy as I could pass out.

My heart started to dance
As she turned around
She gave me a sweet glance
And I followed her to town.

I was trying to decide
Between a good or bad intention
When alas, whoa, stop.....
She went in....the Police Station.

UNTITLED

Trino se encierra en su cuarto
a escribirte un poema de amor
y huela a hule en ese rato
donde no más humea el borrador.

NOCHE BUENA

Es una noche misteriosa y serena,
De los ruidos del mundo esta vacía,
El cielo estaba allí, de amor la llena
con ritmos de alabanza y poesía.

Los astros en el limpio firmamento
destellaban sus ojos y sonrisa,
Mandaban con el viento y la brisa
Los rumores de tan gran evento.

Ven poeta a contar...alza tu voz
Esta noche no es para dormir,
tus pecados Creación va a redimir
Un Niño que ha nacido...el Niño Dios.

NO ESPERES

No esperes que la suerte o el destino
te lleven por la senda de la gloria,
Estudia los peligros del camino
y las lecciones que nos da la historia.

Dios te ha dado un cuerpo tan perfecto
Con una maquinaria, la más fina,
Una gran fuerza...El pensamiento
y la chispa de tu alma que es divina.

Díme has pagado deuda alguna,
has aliviado las penas de tu madre?
Que te crió desde la cuna
que satisfaga tu orgulloso corazón
O las de tu padre
que te dió tu educación?

¿COMO LE PAGO A DIOS?

Cómo le pago a Dios...aquel momento?
en que no tuve yo...ningun derecho,
de que mi madre me diera el sustento
y me alimentara...con su pecho?

Cuando le pagaré...aquella ocasión?
que con su santa luz, la iglesia toda,
Iluminaba con una bendición
la ansiada ceremonia de mi boda?

Por qué le temo tanto, a la muerte
será que mi fe...tengo perdida,
si el haber nacido fué me suerte
no lo puedo pagar, ni con la vida.

Dios no me cobra...y la deuda crece
y yo sé que me espera con paciencia,
y pagaré...cuando mi vida cese
con el impío cristal de mi conciencia.

SOPHIE TUCKER

Diogenes con su linterna
andaba buscando una joya,
que tuviera vida eterna
cuando se encuentra...esta polla.

MAE WEST

Te me vienes en mi mente
Como un trago de "Wine"
si vives eternamente
"Come up and see me sometime."

ZSA ZSA GABOR

Me intriga tanto tu nombre
con tus modos tan extraños,
tan fácil conquistas un hombre
como conquistas los años.

KIM NOVAK

Es la impresión, en mi mente
que vuelve a mi vida la calma
con tu sonrisa inocente
revelas el fondo, de tu alma.

IMPRESIONES II

JOAN CRAWFORD

La fuente de la juventud
que buscaba Ponce de León
la encontraste tú, en Hollywood
y fué mi primer impresión.

MARYLIN MONROE

La impresión que he recibido
me deja la vida inquieta,
con su andar provocativo
y su sonrisa coqueta.

LANA TURNER

Anque mal hable la gente
me deja a mi la impresión,
Dios protege al inocente
cuando es buena su intención.

CYD CHARISSE

Como una obra de arte
Dios te hizo, como ninguna,
muy bien podría yo darte
si tu...me pides la luna.

MIS DOS VISITAS

Dos visitas tuve yo en el hospital
Estando en agonía, y en delirio,
una fué de padre Emmo de San Paul
La otra una en lutada, que era un lirio
Tan seductora, como el pecado mortal.

se acercó a mi cabecera, y muy quieto
Sentí que me besaba, un beso frío
Y me dijo "no tengas miedo
Yo estoy sola y tú...ya eres mío
No digas que no, no hay remedio."

Te vine a buscar y en la puerta
Me dieron tu nombre de una lista.
Nos vamos a Hollywood, tu eres poeta
Yo soy una estrella, soy artista
y quiero un respuesta cierta.

Al tiempo que cedió la calentura
Volví a la razón y la calma,
al ver tan lindísma criatura
Pensé al instante darle mi alma
Que huía de dolor y la amargura.

¿"Buenas días Trinidad cómo has estado?"
oí la voz del Padre,...estaba enfrente
"Yo creo que aquí no has pecado
y vengo a confesarte solamente"
Y se sentó a mi lado.....

Sí padre pequé con el pensamiento;
Le dí mi alma a una estrella,
Se acaba de ir hace un momento
Es una mujer muy bella
y estoy desesperado, no le miento.

"La Virgen de Guadalupe"
es la estrella de tu vida y tu suerte.
Vine porque ayer yo supe
Que venía la enlutada a verte,
Y yo no miento, ella es la "MUERTE."

A VIRGINIA

No es que yo sepa tanto
dígame cuál es tu día,
y le hago una poesía
en el día de su Santo.

Me dijo...no se haga tonto
se le olvidó, la otra vez,
mi día se llega muy pronto
el veintitrés de este mes.

AGUA....Virginia no me digas
los tengo en mi mente impresos
mil poesías y versos
basta que sea mi amiga.

Aunque el día se aproxima
Usted no conoce a Trino
con sólo un trago de vino
todo le que escribe, rima.

Con el licor no lo dudo
Usted no tiene cabeza,
y si cumple su promesa
mañana se muere de crudo

Si me muero, es por tus besos
y las delicias de tu boca
nací poeta....para hacerte versos
cuando tu mirada me provoca.

Y si me escapo de la cruda
y no me muero este día,
Mañana me voy sin duda
si lee estos versos, Sofía.

MI CORAZÓN

Mi corazón esta deshecho
ven, y junta los pedazos
ven, aquí estan mis brazos
para apretarte en mi pecho.

Dáme una invitación
con tus labios de carmín
el aliento de un jazmín
y tu intensa pasión.

Por haberte conocido
con una loca pasión
se me sale el corazón
con solo rozar tu vestido.

Mi vida no es en vano
no te vayas a reír
quiero antes de morir
me dejes besar tu mano.

MAS PURA

El amor es inspiración
con tu alegría secreta
le das la gloria a un poeta
que existe en tu corazón.

La rosa, si la examinas
es símbolo de hermosura
tu eres para, mí, mas pura
pues tu no tienes espinas.

Detrás de tus ojos bellos
está sublime una historia
porque en el fondo de ellos
encontré el cielo y la gloria.

La vida era un problema
porque no te conocía
ahora es un dulce poema
porque sé, que eres mía.

¿POR QUE?

¿Por qué? siendo tú mujer
y yo nada más un hombre
al pronuciar, yo tu nombre
me haces estremecer.

Ven y saca esta pulla
para calmar mi dolor
díme; tú eres mi amor
y yo como siempre, soy tuya.

Si acaso te he despreciado
me ha dado un castigo Dios
pues ando desesperado
cuando no oigo tu voz.

Con aquel amor profundo
como una obra de arte
Dios te mandó a este mundo
y yo sin nada que darte.

PRIMAVERA

Cansado de esperarte, Primavera
Con ese amor tan puro como el cielo
Para besar tu negra cabellera
Y jugar en mis manos con tu pelo.

Como flor que perfuma el ambiente
Te llevaré a mi cuarto, como dueño,
Para dormir contigo, en mi mente
Y besarte mil veces en el sueño.

Si te vas, espero tu regreso
Mi alma te deja la puerta abierta.
Me despido te tí, con sólo un beso
Pero es un beso que te da un poeta.

AL POETA

Canta Poeta al Creador
que con saber tan profundo,
Puso en la vida el amor
Al comenzar este mundo.

Dios no te castigó...al ver
Tu vida tan oprobiosa
Cuando de simple mujer
Hiciste de ella una Diosa.

Porque ella curó tus agravios
Hizo de toda prosa, un verso,
La vacuna fué un beso
Y el remedio, sus labios.

Tu amor fué su sacrificio
Tu vida su mismo aliento
Tu placer fué sufrimiento
Y la ilusión....su paraíso.

DULZURA

Tu tienes en mi concepto
de un jazmín la dulzura
tu perfume, es más perfecto
y por eso estás mas pura.

Es de dos seres humanos
la gloria y el embeleso
yo con mi cara en tus manos
dándome el alma, en un beso.

Jamás yo podré olvidarte
Con tu candor de violeta
como una obra de arte
naciste para un poeta.

Sufro pero no en vano
me considero con suerte
si antes que llegue la muerte
me dejas besar tu mano.

Con mi delirio profundo
de esta pasión tan loca
me creo rey, de todo el mundo
si llego a besar tu boca.

EN EL DIA DE TU SANTO--A LORENZO

Por ser este Día tu Cumpleanos
Busqué un lugai en la tarjeta,
Para desearte muchos años
De Sofia y tu Padre el poeta.
No temas que la gente algun día
Te critiquen por borracho y parrandero
Díles que eras hijo de Sofía
Y de Trino el poeta aventurero.
Contemplando el firmamento
el horizonte se ponía escarlata,
Cuando todo era armonía
Inspirado en el momento
Sale un hermosa Negra--
Mi vecina y adiós poesía.

PARA EL DIA DE TU SANTO--FERNANDO

Brindemos nuestra copa por Fernando
El "Bohemio" de noble corazón,
Que sin hacer alarde
Todo se parece a su padre
En que no se anda emborrachando
No más de corva, como en esta ocasión.

Alzemos nuestra copa por Marcella
La simpática artista de París,
Que no es como nosotros de corriente
Porque ella nunca se desvela
No toma cerveza ni aguardiente
No más toma puro Anís.

Brindemos nuestra copa en este Día
Por Lorenzo y por Sofía
Por todas las buenas amiguitas
Que vinieron el Día de su Santo
Que por Fernando se apuraron tanto
Para cantarle a él "Las Mañanitas."

PARA EL DIA DE TU SANTO
A MARIO

Ahora que no estamos en la casa
Con el día tan bonito y con sol,
No creas que tu día se nos pasa
Aquí está otro soneto en español.

Ahora muy temprano en la mañana
Busqué en mi cartera y no traía
No más un arrugado, cuero de rana
Que te mandamos con gusto en tu Día.

Más y qué sólo se me escapan quejas
Te mando un tiron de las orejas,
Y también un coscorrón de tu Mamá.

Que te portes bien, también te pido
Y no creas que te echamos al olvido
Es todo lo que quiere tu Papá.

PARA ODILA

Si pudiera hacer una pintura
Semejante a la famosa Mona Lisa,
Me reía yo...de la amargura
Y no necesitaba tu sonrisa.

Si tuviera la fuerza de un gigante
para vencer el miedo y el temor
Si tuviera paciencia y fe constante
Necesitaría de tu amor.

Pero no soy pintor ni soy gigante
Mi paciencia y mi fe tengo perdida,
Sólo un beso tuyo....sería bastante
Para darme valor...toda mi vida.

PARA DIA DE TU SANTO
A ODILA

Aunque soy poeta, no soy pobre
Tengo imaginación y te prometo
Que llega a tu corazón este soneto
Con un beso que le dí al sobre.

Dios no cumplirá con mis antojos
Porque yo no siento, no sé llorar,
No voy a la iglesia a rezar
Ni se asoma una lagrima a mis ojos.

Ten calma mujer, no hay agravios
Bajarás como perfume de tu altura,
Al caliz de una flor color de rosa
Yo no soy nada...soy una oruga
Que el tiempo tornará en mariposa
Y los dos juntaremos nuestros labios.

PARA EL DIA DE TU SANTO
A MARGARITA

Era el mes de Octubre y en la fecha
en que nacen las mujeres bellas,
Mi arco es el Iris y mi flecha
Atraviesa el corazón de las estrellas.

Pensé que sin duda yo era poeta
Que Dios me había dado ese don,
Para llegar a tocar la puerta
De tu ingrato y duro corazón.

No obstante mi triste melodía
Me creí el Ruiseñor poblano,
Que quizás algún día llegaría
A darle un beso a tu santo mano.

Pero dios no cumplió con mis antojos
Ni anda consolando a los Cepillos,
Sólo busco la mirada de tus ojos
Para aliviar un poco mis desvíos.

A MI HERMANA MARGARITA

De qué me sirve la ingrata primavera
Con el sol y la mañana tan bonita
Si nadie me llama ni me espera
A tomar café con Margarita.

De qué me sirve levantarme en la mañana
Con ganas de café con mucha hambre
Si ya no veo en la sala a mi hermana
Tejiendo una chamarra con estambre.

El invierno que pasó, yo lo prefiero
Todo blanco de nieve, todo cuajado,
Con la temperatura bajo cero
Y mi hermana platicando del pasado.

Te fuiste como alegre golondrina
Te llevaste tu alegría a otra región
Dejando a Sofía en la cocina.
Con sus penas y su triste corazón.

POEM OF THE WEEK

Larry went to the ball game.
Lucky stiff, for a blind date
He took a peroxided teacher.
When he came back,
He told his pop
He saw the game
From the bleachers.

UNTITLED
Christmast Poem

T o say Merry Christmas
H ere's a Greeting for you--
E very good wish for the New Year, too!

T idings of joy and Christmas cheer
R egal good things are hoped for you here
I ncluding warm wishes most sincere
N ever to fail in the glad New Year.
I t's once again the time to say--
D enoting a future both bright and gay
A nd happy hours come your way
D oubling your joys in each new day.

S incerely, forever may
A ll happiness be yours to stay.
N aturally may you possess
C omplete health and happiness
H our after hour may the future bring
E ndless contentment in everything.
Z ealously seek the acrostic sign--
E very letter, read downward, beginning each line
S pelling who sent you this Christmas time rhyme.

IMPRESIONES

Tongolele

Artista pura, nada falsa
ni falso es su candor,
cuando se luce, descalza,
bailando sobre un tambor.

Rosa Carmina

La tristeza la extermina,
todas las penas derrumba,
el temblor, era de Carmina
que nos bailaba una rumba.

María Félix

Tú me das la impresión
con tu cara celestial,
tu belleza es una visión
el pecado, no es un mal.

Dolores del Río

De México, la Aristocracia
tu talle, es una ilusión
de una rosa, es tu fragancia
y eres noble de corazón.

Toña la Negra

Negra, Pensando en tí
que no lo permita Dios
porque me muero sin tí
si vuelvo....a oir tu voz.

THE GYPSY

I am a Gypsy from Jacksonville.
I tell your fortune for a $ bill.
For two, I make you a poem.
For three, I sing you a song.
For five, I give you a kiss.
For ten, I dance the Can Can.

If you think I am fake,
You can go jump in the Lake.

If you don't like what I sell,
You can go...I better not tell.

UNTITLED

Tu papá no ha cambiado, está lo mismo
Y para alivio de mis males
Ahora está estudiando el hipnotismo
Para aliviar la tristeza a sus comadres.

Buscando en su escritorio una estampilla
Me hallé unos versos y una poesía
Pero ni uno era para Sofía
No más para Juanita y para Eufemia.

Mamá te manda su corazón
Con gusto y muy buen gana,
Papá te manda una coscorrón
Y dos cueros de rana.

EAVESDROPPING

Mama was talking on the phone
With a friend the other day,
I was in another room
But I had the hearing aid.

She was saying to somebody
Trinidad is not so tight,
A girlfriend gave him some money
And let him go at midnite.

A poet has loves to boot
And some of them are very wild,
But none give him any loot.
All he gets is...their smile.

She is on his mind all day
Even when he is at home.`
He calls her Miss Monterrey
And her last name is Poolroom.

TO LITTLE LUCY

Let the storm clean me up
sink my ship without a trace
let the ocean take my loot
these I can replace.

Let me lose a year of time
I will race the sun
or work under a pale star
and get things done.

Let the thunder from above
turn my hut into a blaze,
but don't let me lose your love
for that...I cannot replace.

This is believed to be Dad's last poem.
He wrote it on a card congratulating
Lucy on the birth of her last child;
two days later he died.

TO LUCY

To write you is a pleasure
To make a poem is a cinch
You are a nice looking person
And a real queen every inch.

When you see green on the grass
You know Spring is near
If you see green inside this card
Your birthday must be here.

TO LUCY
On Her Birthday

I promise to write a poem
To you, my only sweetheart,
I realize when I got home
That I forgot to mail the card.

Your day came in with Lent
And I had nothing but water,
Where the inspiration went
To write a poem to my daughter.

Even if you miss the sun
The moonlight or the breeze,
You won't miss in this poem
The eagerness of my kiss.

ANIVERSARIO--A LILA

F ácil se me hizo, y qué trabajo
E n escribirte este verso,
L eelo de arriba para abajo
I ncluyo en el mensaje, un beso
Z ozobrando me animó travieso.

A l celebrar esta ocasión
N o se me hace extraño,
I ntonar de todo corazón
V ivir pasados años
E n que comenzabas a vivir
R isueña en tu primer cumpleanos
S in darte cuenta qué es sufrir,
A hora existen en mi mente
R ecuerdos de aquel cariño puro
O lvidando las penas del presente.

A LOLA

A una boda fuimos, mas no en vano
Ví una mujer gentil y muy hermosa,
Semejante a un jazmín mexicano
Con un semblante de color de rosa.

Pensé que sin duda, era española
Nativa de Madrid o de Valencia,
Quise hablar con ella, pero sola,
Y esperé una chanza con paciencia.

Vestida de crespón, verde esmeralda
Con su talle de juncal palmera,
Me atraía el imán de su mirada
Me intrigaba el saber quién era.

Quién es la Española de tan lindos ojos?
La pregunté a mi mujer por fin,
"Válgame, Trino, ponte los anteojos
Esa es Lola Guzmán la de Agustín."

CELOS

Como quema el sol en la llanura
Y da vida a las hierbas del barbecho,
Se abate mi corazón en la amargura
Y nacen los celos en mi pecho.

Tengo celos de la flor que has cortado
Y a tu lecho llevaste con empeño,
A ponerla un florero a tu lado
Para velar y perfumar tu sueño.

Tengo celos del canto de jilguero
Que dices que viene a despertarte,
Pero yo no soy flor, ni soy florero
Ni tengo alas como ese Cuyumate.

LA MUJER

Teniendo nada que hacer
mi puse aquí a escribir,
queriendo yo a descubrir
qué cosa es la mujer.

Llegué a la conclusión
aunque no es nueva la idea
para mí ninguna es fea
de ellas es mi corazón.

Dios la hizo atractiva
ama siempre a la mujer,
en ella puso el placer
y el secreto de la vida.

Las amo aunque no quiera
las feas, locas o bellas,
y si no fuera por ellas
entonces yo no existiera.

Busca en ellas...el amor
no te guíes por el brillo,
lo mas hermoso es sencillo
si está muda...es mejor.

EN EL DIA DE TU SANTO
A Mi Hermano Fermín Sánchez

Por cada año que tu hayas cumplido
Te deseo veinte más como pintor
En el arte que tú has escogido
De bohemio, dibujante y soñador.

He admirado en las visitas a tu casa
Los rincones llenos de pinturas,
De toros matadores y en la Plaza
Las Reinas en toda su hermosura.

Una veleta empujada por el viento
Surcando los olas del océano,
Arriba el azul del firmamento
Abajo la firma de mi hermano.

No temas que un idiota con su calma
Critique tu trabajo por envidia,
El pintor es un naúfrago del alma
Que vivo se hunde pero no se humilla.

No temas al futuro que algun día
Olviden tu trabajo o tu historia,
La suerte o el destino bien podría
Quitarte el triunfo pero no la Gloria.

Confórmate Fermín, ser firme y fuerte
Ni un paso atrás, no te acobardes,
Tu pintando óleos con aceite
Yo haciendo poesías a las comadres.

A TRINO II

Lo primero que hizo la ingrata
fué comprar esa tarjeta,
para desearte en la pascua
la inspiración de un poeta .

Un sol fuerte de medio día
para ponerte más prieta
tu cara descolorida,
que Diós te abra la puerta
y oigas la melodía.

De una voz vaga y desierta
del corazon de Sofía
y de papá su alma inquieta
que se pasa todo el día
queriendo hacerse poeta.

A TRINO III

Yo amo la poesía y por eso
Tu nombre me inspira,
A mandarte esta tarjeta, con un verso
El mejor de mi lira.

Desde el día que te fuiste
Traigo una pena muy honda
Con un acento muy triste
Como el canto de una alondra.

Como pájaro perdido
Sin más consuelo en el alma
Sin saber en cuál rama
Iré a colgar mi nido

Si me mandas tu carta
Buscaré con fervor
Lo que más me hace falta
Una migaja de amor.

TO TRINO

When you feel lonesome and blue,
Count all the stars in the sky.
It is the times, we think of you
Since the day, you said, "Good-Bye."

When you see the moon so bright
Or feel the touch of the breeze,
Ask the moon every night
Or the wind, for our kiss.

Don't fear the storm, in the brink
Or the high winds in the night.
It is Papa, who took a drink
And wanted to hug you tight.

RECUERDOS

Sólo en México...no más
recuerdos dulces de antaño,
que no olvidaré...jamás
aunque se pasen los años.

El sol tenas encendia
el suelo polvorosa alfombra,
descalso, brincaba y corría
Mis pies buscando la sombra.

Allá en el recodo del río
una joven recatada,
en la orilla se bañaba
bajo un árbol sombrío.

El sol con ojos traviesos
cuando ella se descuidaba,
le quemaba con sus besos
ni una nube se estorbaba.

Se alza un poco la enagua
al verla tan linda, tal vez
queria yo, volverme agua
para acariciar sus pies.

LOS INDIOS DE MI PUEBLO

Los indios van bajando por la cuesta
Con rumbo a la Parroquia, a ver al Cura,
Y pedirle un Crucifijo, ya en la fiesta
Con el baile, atraer la lluvia.

Año por año, en la misma fecha
Se escasea el agua torrencial,
Y temen que se queme la cosecha
Sin la ayuda del Cristo Parroquial.

Los indios que jamás habían visto
Ni esperaban tremenda tempestad,
Se preparan a llevar a Jesucristo
Y devolverlo a la Parroquia en la cuidad.

¿Nos presta la Imagen de Nuestra Santa Madre?
Y dijo el Cura, ¿Qué, no sirvió el Crucifijo?
Sí padre, pero queremos enseñarle
Todos los destrozos que nos hizo su Hijo.

A MI PATRIA

Patria, te pido perdón
y al cielo extiendo mis brazos,
te guardo en mi corazón
aunque está hecho pedazos.

Por un falso paraíso
soy ahora americano,
si el destino así lo quiso
por dentro, soy mexicano.

Pero Patria, no lloremos
un hijo no vas a perder,
cuando yo vuelva a nacer
te prometo, allá nos vemos.

A MI PUEBLO NATAL

Brindémos por Piedras Negrás, Coahúila
La Cuidad Norteña,
que eternamente nos enseña
Nos cuida y nos vigila.

A vivir como un cristiano
Donde el cariño es más sincero,
Donde se entrega la mano
Se entrega el corazón entero.

Con la planta de agua potable
La gente es más amable,
Los problemas aún, no están resueltos.

Aunque siempre han sido pocos
Aquí no hoy hospital de locos,
Porque como yo, pues andan sueltos.

"VIVA MEXICO"

Fue un sueño...no lo dudo.
Como hablo, hasta dormido,
no puedo quedarme mudo
de este sueño, que no han oído.

Oye, Trino...qué soñaste?
con una voz muy templada,
"VIVA MEXICO" gritaste
y casi en la madrugada.

Soñé....que me fusilaban
en frente de un paredón
los soldados se formaban
yo rezaba....una oración.

Mi conciencia hablaba, en vano
"tú no eres traicionero
si te hiciste ciudadano
no lo hiciste por dinero".

La angustia que yo pasé
vendado allí....como ciego,
"Preparen...Apunten...Fuego"
Entonces fué cuando yo grité.

MI CONCIENCIA

Mi conciencia no duerme es una bruja
Que martiriza mi pobre corazón,
Si yo pudiera quitarle esa aguja
La conquistaba, a tenerme compasión.

Pensé que sin duda era mujer
Traidora como todas las demás
Mientras supe cumplir con mi deber
La ingrata me dejó en paz.

Con los años y mi buena suerte
Me hallé una morena muy bonita
Simpática, joven y tan fuerte
Con el tiempo le busco una chambita.

Entonces mi conciencia sin tardar
Me dijo al oído: Oye Artista
El don de la mujer es: solo amar
Y aquí traigo mi aguja siempre lista.

YO

Soy de dos almas opuestas, heredero
Del indio triste y resignado,
Del español blásfemo y renegado
Do noble corazón y pendenciero.

Vengo de una esfera celestial
Mansión de las estrellas y cometas,
Donde existe un paraíso eternal
De donde vienen todos los poetas.

Quiero pasar el resto de mi vida
En alta mar y contigo a solas
Para escuchar de Dios la bienvenida
Y el magestuoso tumbo de la olas.

Voy a morir cuando se llegue el día
En la orilla del mar mirando al cielo
Para ver que se aleja el alma mía
Como gaviota que remonta el vuelo.

LEVANTATE

El amor es natural,
es la ley del Universo.
Tu boca me atrae, a un beso
amarnos no es un mal.

Dios podrá separar
la marea con el mar
sólo Dios puede evitar
que nos dejemos de amar.

El amor es poesía
el tiempo es eternidad
tú eres la noche, yo el día
tú sofía....yo, Trinidad.

Unidos eternamente
en los lazos del destino,
por qué no pierdo la mente,
y agarro otro camino?

No es castigo de Dios
ni que haya perdido la fe
es que quiero oír tu voz:
Levántate, quieres café?

EL GENIO

Era un Domingo, por cierto
me acuerdo como un sueño,
andábamos por un desierto
cuando se aparaece "un Genio."

Se dirigió a mi mujer
soy un genio, no el Rey Midas,
yo te voy a conceder
una cosa que tú me pidas.

Mi mujer no titubeó
Quiero que me hagas más joven
20 años, quisiera yo
cansada estoy, que me estorben.

Vuelve el rejoj para atrás
no le tomas algún daño
cuenta bien, ni menos, ni mas
cada vuelta es un año.

No la creía capaz
que Sofia embelece
movio el reloj para atrás
a comenzar nueva vida.

La miraba más bonita
cuando a un espejo se asoma,
estaba más delgadita
ya no era la misma paloma.

Y pegó un grito asustada
mis hijos, no están por hay?
Ellos se volvieron nada
te acaban de decir "Good bye."

Confórmate mi prietita
y nunca envidies, jamás,
eres mas feliz ahorita
que 20 años para atrás.

A MI MUJER

Ahora que ella se halla ausente
me he preocupado...pero un poco
la tengo muy cerca...en mi mente
aunque ella me diga, que estoy loco.

Hay muchas mujeres en el mundo
a pesar de los años..son bellezas,
que saben querer, con amor profundo
y no se quejan...mi mujer es de esas.

Quisiera enviarle perfumadas flores
en mi mente componerle una canción
para decirle y cantarle mis amores.

Mas ya que sólo se me escapan quejas
le remito a mi bien...un coscorrón
y un soberbio tirón de las orejas.

MI NEGRA

Y acaso tú me dejas
sería yo muy feliz
me invitaron para Téxas
puedo arreglar mi veliz.

Sin pensar, le contesté
si ella lo necesita,
puede irse desde ahorita
y luego, fuí y me acosté.

Que sorpresa al oír su voz
cuando estaba yo soñando,
Papá me están esperando
y díle a Virginia "Adiós."

Para no volverme loco
me puse a hacer estos versos,
pensando que, poco a poco
me hacen falta sus besos.

Díme negra, por qué te fuiste
me quieres seguir un mal,
quieres que el vulgo me llame
"El poeta de arrabal."

ANIVERSARIO

Muy pronto se llegó el Aniversario
El catorce de Mayo es el Día,
Que cumplo diez años de Notario
Y cuarenta casado con Sofía.

En secreto se juntaron los Cepillos
A darle a su papá una sorpresa
Para aliviar un poco de sus desvíos
Y quitarle de la mente su tristeza.

Si confunden la tristeza con la calma
Mi mente habita el mar, como gaviota,
El poeta es un naúfrago del alma
Que vivo se hunde pero muerto flota.

Mi animo se hallaba por el suelo
Pero vuelve a volar con nuevos bríos,
Como un ave que remonta el vuelo
Ahora que vinieron los Cepillos.

TEN PACIENCIA
SE MAS DISCRETA

Ten paciencia se mas discreta
No te hallas otro hombre, piensa bien
Que te haga verso como un poeta
Y lo hagas sufrir con tu desdén.

Confórmate mujer, no hay que llorar
Pronto llegaremos a la meta,
Tu como miel para endulzar
El amargo corazón de un poeta.

No soy rico pero soy un mago
Tengo imaginación y otra cosa,
Te gustan los versos que yo te hago
Y eso vale más que ser mi esposa.

Por ser ahora día de tu Santo
El billete que te mando esta vez,
Vale más que lo pongas en el Banco
Porque si no lo gastas en el Kress.

UNTITLED

Tiene Sofía la buena intención
De llevarme a Detroit al Hospital,
Para que me hagan una operación
Y me curen una vez de mi mal.

Sofía quiere, la muy ingrata
Que me pongan un corazón nuevo,
La cara de Rock Hudson y luego
Una garganta como de un Sinatra.

PARA EL DIA DE TU SANTO
A Sofía

Me criticas porque soy borracho
pero eso es tu deber.
Te quiero porque al fin soy macho
Y también porque eres mi mujer.

Me criticas porque no trabajo
Por huevón, porque soy muy pillo,
Me paso la vida, fumando tabaco
Y durmiendo de día como un grillo.

PARA TU MAMA
En El Día De Su Santo

Busqué una mujer que no comiera
Y Díos me castigó por egoista,
Me mandó una buena cocinera.
Para hacer antojitos anda lista.

Busqué una mujer joven y sana
Que me diera cuando viejo, buen servicio
Tengo una que temprano en la mañana
Pone el café y también la televisión.

Me hallé una con tan buena suerte
Simpática, morena y tan fuerte
Que quise ponerla a trabajar.

Pero entonces me dijo: No me apuro
Por eso me casé con un burro
Que me dé dinero que gastar.

A SOFIA
En el día de su Santo

Busqué inspiracion en las estrellas
Y la noche estaba muy oscura,
Busqué una flor blanca y pura
Y el invierno acabo con ellas.

Entonces busqué en mi cartera
Y me hallé tu retrato y tu sonrisa,
El invierno se cambió en primavera
El frío en perfumada brisa.

No hay persona enamorada
Ni hallas otro hombre....busca bien
Que no hagas feliz con tu mirada
Que lo hagas sufrir con tu desdén.

Nos vamos a un verde paraíso
A pasar el invierno en la playa,
A bailar al ritmo del Calipso
Al son de un bongo y mi guitarra.

PARA SOFIA
EN EL DIA DE SU SANTO

Qué quieres, como un presente
para el día de su Santo?
Y me contesta, la inocente:
Un verso, si me quieres tanto.

Díme si tengo los ojos
como los que tiene Lola,
si mis labios estan rojos
como de una española?

Si hallaste en mí la melodía
de una isla tropical
como la voz de María
o Juanita Villarreal?

Si me soñaste muy niña
bajo un cielo dorado,
como soñaste a Virginia
como a un ángel a tu lado?

Y díme todas tus quejas
como le escribiste a Eufemia
cuando se fué para Téxas
en aquel dulce poema?

Siempre que te beso yo
se te olvida en un segundo,
cuando Frances te besó
tu fuiste al otro mundo.

Busqué mi bola de cristal
para pedirle un consejo,
y no me sentí tan mal
me dijo, no estás tan viejo.

Anda y díle a Sofía
que aún te faltan veinte años
para hacerle una poesía
en cada uno de sus cumpleaños.

8

Evangelina Vigil, in her introduction to my book of poems, points out that we are poets of "two distinct generations," one the classical style of Mexican poets and writers, and the other more influenced by the "voz del pueblo," a style of Chicano and black poets of Detroit Horizon In Poetry. We both write about friends, about the loves of our lives, important places and moments in our histories, but my father trancends the socio-political realities of his time.

There are several notable poets who are father and son; however, I am told we are the only father and son poets who share the first and last name. Being published with him is my way of honoring the memory of my father. He will be remembered by those who knew him and more importantly, he will not be forgotten by those who never knew him, his grandchildren and great-grandchildren.

Trinidad Sánchez, Jr.
Detroit, Michigan
6/17/1984

My favorite poet is Salvador Díaz Míron and the poems 'TO GLORIA' - I can recite from memory...in this case I am not a poet like him, but I am more romantic. My idol after God is the woman. I owe my life and the happiness of all my family to Our Lady of Guadalupe, she is the owner of my Faith." 1/15/1964

Papa captured his own spirit in this quote from a letter to a friend. Salvador D. Miron may have been his favorite poet, but Papa's library contained books by other Mexican and Latino poets such as Juan de Dios Peza, Antonio Plaza, Ruben Dario, Manuel M. Flores, Manuel Acuña, Jose Maria Gabriel y Galan, Maria Luisa Villoro, Sor Juana Ines de la Cruz, Amado Nervo and Manuel Gutierrez Najera.

Papa was not a man of formal education, able to attend school only to the 6th grade; however, he did develop an appreciation for the poets of his era and their writings. He also enjoyed reading Robert Frost.

In a copy of a letter to Talleres de 'El Libro Espanol' in Mexico, around 1965, Papa inquired about the possibility of publishing a book of his poems "...his family and friends encouraged him to publish a book." He explained in the same letter that he did so"...not so much for money, but as a remembrance of the verses that he had dedicated to family and close friends."

In a copy of another letter written to me, Papa wrote, "I make a poem almost every day, mostly in Spanish. By the time I retire, in three years, I will have enough to publish a book or make a big fire."

Included in these letters that Papa wrote to me were always copies of his most recent poems. I have saved them, hoping someday to publish them, fulfilling that dream of my father.

It was in 1981, upon my return to Detroit, my dear mother presented me with the collection of Dad's poems. At the time she indicated Papa had written poetry since he was a young man, courting her with poems and love letters. It was not until the late fifties, however, that he began to keep carbon copies of his poems.

INTRODUCTION

This selection of my father's poems is from a collection of his poetry that has been passed on to me by my dear mother after she discovered my serious interest in poetry.

Writing poetry was a pastime from his work as proprietor of THE MONTEREY POOLROOM, located on Wilson Street a few blocks from where we all grew up. He was the first Mexican to own his own business in Pontiac, Michigan. As a child, I recall staying up late to watch the Jack Paar Show. I remember seeing Papa sitting at the dining room table writing his poems late into the evening.

Papa's poems were frequently published in the newspaper EL HERALDO and the St. Vincent De Paul Church Bulletin. After his death in 1965, a selection was published in EL QUETZAL EMPLUMECE, published by the Mexican American Cultural Center, San Antonio, Texas.

I often explain to children I teach that I did not appreciate the poetry of my father when I was growing up. I do recall, however, Papa's love for the dramatic flair as he recited his poems to gatherings of friends and family on the weekends or holidays. Papa at mealtimes was his best, sitting at the head of the table retelling the humorous stories and events from his past.

Cumpleaños, birthdays, in the Mexican tradition are celebrations of life. They are special days which Papa called attention to with his poetry. It was his way of entering into the celebration and sharing this gift...de todo corazon.

"Mi poeta favorita es Salvador Díaz Míron y las poesias
'A GLORIA' catorce cuartetos, los puedo recitar de memoria . . .
en este caso yo no seria poeta como el, pero si soy más romantico.
Mi idolo despues de Dios es la mujer. A nuestra Señora de
Guadalupe le debo yo la vida y la felicidad de toda mi familia,
ella es duena de mi Fe." 1/15/1964

39 PARA DIA DE TU SANTO A ODILA
40 PARA EL DIA DE TU SANTO A MARIO
41 PARA EL DIA DE TU SANTO - FERNANDO
42 EN EL DIA DE TU SANTO A LORENZO
43 DULZURA
44 PRIMAVERA
44 AL POETA
45 POR QUE?
46 MAS PURA
47 MI CORAZON
48 A VIRGINIA
49 MIS DOS VISITAS
50 IMPRESIONES II
52 COMO LE PAGO A DIOS
53 NOCHE BUENA
53 NO ESPERES
54 ALMOST
54 UNTITLED
55 SIACASO VUELVES
56 IF YOU COME BACK

CONTENIDO

5   Introduction by Trinidad Sánchez, Jr.

8   PHOTO: TRINIDAD & SOFIA SANCHEZ
9   PARA SOFIA EN EL DIA DE SU SANTO
10 A SOFIA EN EL DIA DE SU SANTO
11 PARA EL DIA DE SU SANTO, A Sofia
11 PARA TU MAMA En El Dia de su Santo
12 TEN PACIENCIA SE MAS DESCRETA
12 UNTITLED
13 ANIVERSARIO
14 PHOTO: SOFIA SANCHEZ
15 MI NEGRA
16 A MI MUJER
17 EL GENIO
18 LEVANTATE
19 YO
20 MI CONCIENCIA
21 VIVA MEXICO
22 A MI PATRIA
22 A MI PUEBLO NATAL
23 LOS INDIOS DE MI PUEBLO
24 RECUERDOS
25 TO TRINO
26 A TRINO II
26 A TRINO III
27 EN EL DIA DE TU SANTO A Mi Hermano Fermin Sánchez
28 LA MUJER
29 A LOLA
29 CELOS
30 ANIVERSARIO A LILA
31 TO LUCY
31 TO LUCY On Her Birthday
32 TO LITTLE LUCY
33 EAVESDROPPING
34 THE GYPSY
34 UNTITLED
35 IMPRESIONES
36 POEM OF THE WEEK
36 UNTITLED Christmas Poem
37 PHOTO: TRINIDAD WITH HIS SISTER MARGARITA
37 A MI HERMANA MARGARITA
38 PARA EL DIA DE TU SANTO A MARGARITA
39 PARA ODILA

POESIAS
DE
TRINIDAD V. SANCHEZ

with Introduction by
Trinidad Sánchez, Jr.

Pecan Grove Press • St. Mary's University
San Antonio, Texas

Mail Order Form for Books & CD's by Trinidad Sánchez Jr.

Books	Price
Why Am I So Brown?"	$15.00
Poems by Father & Son	$15.00
Compartiendo de la Nada	$5.00
Authentic Chicano Food is Hot!	$12.00
Jalapeno Blues - Available Winter 2002	$15.00
Pre-Order and reserve your copy now!	

C.D.s	Price
Why Am I So Brown?	$15.00
Greatest Hits/Los Mas Grandes Exitos	$15.00

Payable in U.S. Funds ONLY. No cash orders accepted.
Postage and handling $2.00 per item.
Prices, postage and handling charges may change without notice.
Credit card orders, Mastercard or VISA accepted.
Please allow 4 to 6 weeks for delivery.

Please bill my credit card:

VISA #	
Mastercard #	
Expiration Date:	
Signature:	

Address & phone number MUST be the same as the billing statement.

Send order form, money order or checks to:
Trinidad Sánchez, Jr.
3480 Grape Street
Denver, CO 80207
For more information call: (303) 388-POET

Name	
Address	
City	
State	
Zip Code	
Telephone Number	

Order Total	$
Shipping and Handling	$
Sales Tax (Colorado 7.8%)	$
Total Amount Due	$